FIRENZE
MVSEI

National Archaeological Museum

edited by
Anna Maria Esposito
and
Maria Cristina Guidotti

GIUNTI

The section on the Etruscan, Greek and Roman Collections
edited by Anna Maria Esposito includes contributions
by Anna Rastrelli on Funerary Sculpture
and Antonella Romualdi on Bronze Statuary.
M. Cygielman, F. Curti, G. De Tommaso, O. Paoletti and E. Paribeni
are thanked for their scientific consultation.

Graphics: Franco Bulletti
Cover design: Laura Belforte *and* Fabio Filippi

Editorial manager: Claudio Pescio
Editor: Augusta Tosone
Translation: Catherine Frost

Photographic credits: Tuscan Archaeological Heritage,
Consorzio Pisa Ricerche *and* Foto Rabatti-Domingie, Florence

Editorial production by Giunti Gruppo Editoriale, Florence
ISBN 88-09-01347-6

Contents

Idolino of Pesaro

ENOUGH BOOKS have been written about the public museums in Florence run by the Fine Arts and Historic Works Commission to fill a large library. This is hardly surprising when one considers that the artistic heritage preserved in our museums has been famous throughout the world for centuries. For hundreds of years writers, scholars and travellers of every nationality and country have been attempting to describe all that the Florentine museums contain. They have made great efforts to explain why these museums are so fascinating, and to lead a path through paintings and sculptures for both the uninformed but willing visitor and the refined and jaded intellectual.

Over time, however, the museums have altered their aspect and their layout, the exhibitions have been arranged in new ways, the collections have been enriched (or impoverished). Attributions of works in the museums have also changed, restorations have transformed the appearance of many pieces, the rise and fall of aesthetic tendencies have led to reorganisation and the exhibition of differing works. All these things are constantly taking place within the public collections because museology and the history of art, like any intellectual endeavour, are in a constant state of progress and transformation. This explains why the literature surrounding the Florentine museums (like that of any of the world's great art collections) is so immense, and in a process of continual updating and change.

The perfect, definitive guide to a museum, any museum, does not and cannot exist.

The premise seems obvious, but is nonetheless necessary in order to understand the point of the publication introduced by these lines. From the moment when, in accordance with the application of the Ronchey law 4/93, the Giunti publishing house group took over the running of the support services within the Florentine museum system, it was decided to start at once on a standardised series of illustrated guides. These guides, displaying the cuneiform flower of Firenze Musei *on the cover, guarantee that at the year of publication the state of each museum is exactly that described in the guide.*

Certain things are obviously necessary if a museum guide is to aspire to reliability, official standing and at the same time enjoy a wide distribution: accuracy of information, high quality reproductions, an easily manageable format, a reasonable cost and – not least – a clearly written text (without, naturally, being banal or lacking in precision). Readers will judge for themselves if the guide which follows this introduction reaches these standards. I have no doubt that this will be a serious and committed judgement, just as myself and the Publisher of this guide have been serious and committed in attempting to meet the cultural needs of whoever visits our museums in the best way and with every possible care.

Head of the Fine Arts
and Historic Works Commission
of Florence, Pistoia and Prato
(Antonio Paolucci)

THE NATIONAL ARCHAEOLOGICAL MUSEUM

ONE OF THE SUREST indications of the good state of health of a Museum consists of the availability of efficient, updated and scientifically correct instruments of diffusing knowledge, on both the specialized level and that of the average visitor.

Catalogues, then (but also publications for children, requiring equally careful preparation) and guides, such as that which the reader is about to glance through, compiled by persons who have long been involved in the Museum and are still involved in it, for specific tasks as well as more general scientific interest.

The multitude of authors is not surprising. Archeology occupies in fact a central position not only as regards Tuscan museums but also within the complex of Italian museums of antiquities, starting from the simple fact of the extension and quality of the pieces exhibited.

As explained in the following introductory pages, the present-day Archaeological Museum unites collections differing in origin and subject, from the Egyptian ones (the most important in Italy after those of Turin) to a substantial portion of the Medici and Lorraine collections split up after the Unification of Italy, as well as a panorama of what specialized research has brought to light in over a century of work, both within the boundaries of Tuscany and outside of it.

Around this group of antiquities the Archaeological Department has been working intensely in recent years, to arrive in the near future at more complete and better illustrated exhibition. Inevitably, this will lead to the need to revise this guide again, but – we are certain – it will be worth the trouble.

The Director
of the Tuscan Archaeological Heritage
(Angelo Bottini)

THE NATIONAL ARCHAEOLOGICAL MUSEUM of Florence was inaugurated in 1870 by King Vittorio Emanuele II, within the context of the reorganization of Florentine museums carried out while Florence was the capital of Italy. In the Etruscan Museum, established alongside the existing Egyptian Museum (1885), were placed the Medici and Lorraine Collections of ancient art, containing works of great value, not only Etruscan but also Greek and Roman. After a ten years' stay in the Educatorio di Foligno in Via Faenza, the collections were moved to the 17th century Palazzo della Crocetta, built in 1619-21 by G. Parigi on the site of a Casino constructed by Lorenzo the Magnificent, as a residence for Maria Maddalena, the sister of Cosimo II de' Medici. To allow the unfortunate princess, "deformed in her limbs", to reach the nearby church of Santissima Annunziata without going outside, a long corridor was built (now used for the Museum's glyptic collection), ending in a balcony overlooking the church where the princess could attend mass unseen. In 1889 King Umberto I created the Royal National Museum of Antiquities in Rome and transformed the Florence Etruscan Museum into the Royal Central Museum

Tholos from Casale Marittimo
(Monumental Garden)

of Etruscan Civilization. Subsequently some of the ancient material kept in the Uffizi and elsewhere in Florence was brought to Palazzo della Crocetta – the *Idolino* and other bronzes from the classic age (1890), some ancient marble statues, jewelry (1895), and the glyptic and numismatic collection (1897). In the same year a new section was inaugurated by Luigi Adriano Milani, director of the Museum since 1894. This was the Topographical Museum of Etruria which, through materials coming from excavations on the sites of great Etruscan cities, proposed to illustrate "the origins of a people, its relations and connections with other peoples, to trace its very private history, its domestic life, its industrial activity..." (Milani). In the garden, opened to the public in 1902, several tombs found at the time were reconstructed with original materials, for the purpose of documenting Etruscan funerary architecture (shaft tombs, *tholoi*, chamber tombs, etc.). In the "Roman courtyard" were placed fragments of architecture coming from urban excavations in Florence, assembled to form "ideal" monuments. With the purchase of the former Palazzo Innocenti at the corner of Piazza Santissima Annunziata and Via Gino Capponi in 1942 the Museum was enlarged and a monumental entrance was opened on the piazza. The 1966 flood caused immense damage to the archaeological collections and the building itself. Although the damaged objects have been entirely salvaged through years of work carried out by the Tuscan Archaeological Department Restoration Center, the exhibition halls have been restored only partially, so that still today entire sections of the Museum remain inaccessible and thousands of invaluable works are deposited in storage.

Chamber tomb from Orvieto (Monumental Garden)

The Florence Egyptian Museum, second in Italy only to the more famous one of Turin, is housed in the Archaeological Museum. A first core of Egyptian antiquities existed in Florence already in the 18th century in the Medicean Collections, but during the 19th century it was substantially augmented when the Grand Duke of Tuscany Leopoldo II purchased in 1842 a collection of Egyptian finds (approximately 1,400 pieces) from Giuseppe Nizzoli, Chancellor of the Austrian Consulate in Egypt. Already for years European diplomats in Egypt had been collecting antiquities, to be sold in their homelands where they were to form the basis of Europe's great Egyptian museums. The Grand Duke also financed, in collaboration with Charles X King of France, a scientific expedition to Egypt in the years 1828 and 1829, led by Jean-François Champollion, the famous decipherer of hieroglyphs, and by Ippolito Rosellini from Pisa, who was to become the father of Italian Egyptology. The two scholars had met during Champollion's visit to Florence to examine the Nizzoli Collection just purchased by the Grand Duke. A close friendship ensued, with Rosellini soon becoming the faithful disciple of the French Egyptologist. Together they planned a scientific expedition to Egypt, to further the study of hieroglyphs and collect relics of Egyptian civilization. The numerous objects collected during the journey, in archaeological excavations as well as by purchasing material on local markets, were equally shared between Paris (the Louvre) and Florence (about 2,200 pieces). Another collection of Egyptian finds was purchased by Leopoldo II in 1832. It consisted of approximately 850 objects collected by the Sienese physician and traveler Alessandro Ricci.

In 1855 the Florence Egyptian Museum was officially inaugurated when

Egyptian chariot

these collections were brought together in the former convent of the Foligno nuns in Via Faenza. In 1889, after some decades without major changes, the young Piemontese Egyptologist Ernesto Schiaparelli, future director of the Turin Egyptian Museum, was assigned the task of moving the Florence Egyptian Museum to its present site in Via Colonna, in association with the Archaeological Museum. The Egyptian Museum was inaugurated in 1883 in the presence of King Umberto and Queen Margherita of Savoia, as recalled in the hieroglyphs painted on the lintels of rooms II and III. With Schiaparelli the Florentine Egyptian collections were enriched again, very substantially this time, by his excavations and purchases made in Egypt before moving to Turin, leaving the Museum without an Egyptologist up until the 1930s. The last group of collections received by the Florence Egyptian Museum consists of donations from individuals and scientific institutes. Particularly important are the finds donated by the Florence Papyrology Institute, coming from excavations conducted in Egypt from 1934 to 1939, preceded by the Newman donation (1919) and followed by the Wilson-Barker legacy (1948).

At present the Florence Egyptian Museum contains over 15,000 objects, distributed over eleven rooms and two storage deposits. The exhibition rooms have been substantially renovated. Schiaparelli's old arrangement is gradually being replaced by a new one, based on the principle of chronological and, when possible, topographical order.

Roman courtyard

EGYPTIAN COLLECTIONS
by Maria Cristina Guidotti

***Male head
of statuette***

Old Kingdom,
V dynasty

Quartzite
Height 13.2
Inv. no. 5638

This male head was part of a statue of rather small size, probably destined to funerary use. The head is adorned by a short wig covering the ears and framing the finely modeled face.

The type of wig and the admirable style in which the face is carved indicate the probable dating.

Entrance Hall

A visit to the Egyptian Museum starts at the foot of the stairway leading to the first floor, where a naos, the base of a column with an Isiatic procession carved in relief and some sarcophagi are placed.

The naos comes from the temple dedicated to Isis, built in Ptolemaic times on the island of Philae near Assuan, now disassembled and reconstructed on a nearby island to save it from being submerged by the waters of Lake Nasser.

It was brought to Florence by the expedition of Ippolito Rosellini, a portrait bust of whom is placed at the top of the first ramp of stairs. The original of this sculpture is in the garden of the Cairo Egyptian Museum, among the busts of the world's greatest Egyptologists.

GIUSEPPE ANGELELLI
The French-Tuscan Expedition to Egypt

1850
Oil on wood
230×347

The large painting at the entrance to the exhibition halls portrays the members of the French-Tuscan Expedition led by Jean-François Champollion and Ippolito Rosellini, shown dressed in Oriental style against the background of the ruins of the Temple of Karnak. In the foreground are some objects brought back by the expedition and now present in the Museum. The standing figure wearing a white mantle is Rosellini. Seated next to him is Champollion holding a scimitar.

The figure in the shadow against the background is a self-portrait of the painter, Giuseppe Angelelli, one of the members of the expedition.

Among the other Italian and French personages is the Sienese Alessandro Ricci, the first on the left, viewed from behind.

Room I

Dedicated to Ernesto Schiaparelli, this room contains materials from the Prehistoric Age to the Middle Kingdom. In the display cases are numerous flintstones dating from the Paleolithic to the Aeneolithic Age, and pottery of various types such as the vases from the Naqada II culture (3500-3000 BC) decorated with rowboats, banners, ostriches, plants, etc. Noteworthy are the series of so-called "cosmetics palettes" in various shapes: fish, antelopes, geometric forms. Among the material datable to the Old Kingdom the models of two servants, a woman grinding grain and another brewing beer, are famous, although heavily repainted in the last century. Among the stone vases on display are two alabaster ones with the cartouches of Pharaohs Unas (5th dynasty) and Merenra (6th dynasty) engraved on them. There are also numerous stone funerary stelae, of which the Florence Egyptian Museum possesses a rich collection.

Fish-shaped cosmetics palette

Prehistoric Age

Schist
Length 19.3
Inv. no. 8111

The palette, in the shape of a fish, was used to pulverize red and yellow ochre. The presence of a hole for hanging indicates a funerary use.

Model of a woman grinding grain

Old Kingdom, V dynasty

Painted limestone
Length 45
Inv. no. 3811

This statuette represents a woman, wearing a striped wig with a ribbon on her forehead, kneeling in the act of grinding a cereal of some kind. The grains come out of a sack held between her knees, and the white flour heaps up in front of the grindstone.

Statue of unknown pharaoh

Middle Kingdom,
XII dynasty

Pink granite
Height 120
Inv. no. 1792

This unknown pharaoh is depicted in a posture typical of royal statues from the 12th dynasty. Seated on a chair, whose dedicatory inscription has been deleted and re-engraved on the base, the pharaoh, wearing the pleated skirt called *scendit*, rests his arms on his thighs. The head and the right arm are missing.

A ritual band held by the pharaoh in his right hand, now lost, remains.
The statue was expropriated over a thousand years after its creation by Pimay, a dignitary of Pharaoh Psammetichos I (26th dynasty), who dedicated it to the memory of his father Sheshonq, prince of the city of Busiris.

Room II

Objects from the Middle Kingdom and the Second Intermediate Period are displayed in this room. Noteworthy in addition to the funerary stelae is the stele commemorating a military campaign led by Pharaoh Sesostris I (12th dynasty), with the images of prisoners, symbolic of the vanquished cities. Other interesting objects are the various wooden models of servants, boats and female statuettes, the so-called "concubines of the dead". Showcase 6 contains the faïence statuette of a hippopotamus and some ivory amulets propitious to hunting, shaped like knives or boomerangs with images of fantastic animals carved on them.

Funerary stele of Ibi

Middle Kingdom
Second Intermediate Period

Painted sandstone
Height 50
Inv. no. 2512

Engraved on the rounded top of this funerary stele is the hieroglyphic that means eternity, flanked by two *udjat* eyes for protection. The deceased Ibi, Master of the Palace bedchamber, is standing in front of a table bearing the funeral offerings: meat, vegetables, bread and amphorae.

The text in hieroglyphs contains a formula for offerings and the names of relatives of the deceased.

ROOM III

Room III is dedicated to the 18th dynasty (New Kingdom). The first section contains a set of models of vases and tools (showcase 13) which formed half of the material taken from Queen Hatscepsut's tomb in the Valley of the Kings. The other er half is in Paris, at the Louvre, brought there by Champollion, who shared the entire treasure with Rosellini. Facing this is a very good Fayyūm Portrait, datable to the 4th century AD, presently out of chronological context pending definitive collocation.

Outstanding among the 18th dynasty statuary are the headless statue of Pharaoh Thothmes III, wearing the characteristic costume of the Sed festival of jubilation (30th year of reign) ; the probable Head of Queen Ty, wife of Amenophis III, and a splendid bust of a woman from post-Amarnian art. On the back wall are fragments of decorative scenes from painted tombs, coming from the necropolis at Thebes.

The second section of Room III is dedicated to material from everyday life.

A famous chariot found disassembled and almost intact in a Theban tomb from the 18th dynasty is displayed here, along with a bow that was part of its equipment. Throughout the 19th century the chariot was thought to be Asiatic, not Egyptian. However, comparison with Pharaoh Tutankhamen's chariots from the same period has confirmed that it is Egyptian, finer and more elegant than the Asiatic models, designed to be drawn by two horses and carry two persons, the driver and the warrior. Traces of wear show that it was really used, for either hunting or warfare, by the owner of the tomb where it was found.

In the same room are numerous jars for cosmetics, pomades and kohl ; musical instruments and writing materials, including fragments of stone or broken pottery called ostraka, used for notes, school exercises, and lists for which papyrus was too expensive.

Among the furniture is a chair with footstool (showcase 26) and the headrests that supported the neck during sleep.

The headrest consists of an elongated base, a grooved stem and a curved "cushion" that was padded with fabric.

The "cushion" is decorated at both ends by the face of the daemon Bes carved in bas-relief.

Bes was responsible for protecting the sleeper, or the deceased, against evil spirits.

Wooden headrest
New Kingdom,
XIX dynasty

Wood
Height 25
Inv. no. 2340

Fayyūm portrait of a woman

Roman Period,
4ᵗʰ century AD

Painted wood
Height 32,5
Inv. no. 2411

The panel portrays the face of a young woman, her hair arranged in curly locks surmounted by a little topknot.
She wears pearl earrings and a necklace of dark stones.
Portraits of this kind were placed over the face of the mummy in Roman times.

Head of Queen Ty

New Kingdom, XVIII dynasty
Gray granite
Height 45
Inv. no. 7659

The head still bears the lower part of a crown, indicating that the statue portrayed the queen in the form of a goddess.
The diadem probably consisted of the solar disk with cow's horns, typical of the goddess Isis.
On the brow is the erect uraeus, the cobra symbolic of royalty.
The statue has been identified as that of Queen Ty on the basis of stylistic elements.

17

Statue of Huemascia and his wife Baket, repeated twice

New Kingdom, XVIII dynasty
Limestone
Height 62
Inv. no. 1802

The scribe Huemascia, wearing a wig and a long skirt, is shown seated on a high-backed bench, in the act of embracing his wife Baket (whose name is engraved on the front of her tunic), represented twice, to the left and the right of the scribe. On the back and sides of the bench are portrayed the nine children of the couple, with their names. The repetition of the figure of Baket, quite rare in Egyptian statuary, can be explained only as a desire for symmetry in portraying the couple.

ROOMS IV-V

Rooms IV and V contain material from the New Kingdom coming from various localities. In addition to a few finds datable to the Amarnian period, the first room contains a box with four compartments for the four canopic jars of the deceased Takharu (showcase 7).

Noteworthy are the funeral stelae of Ramses, of excellent quality, and of Takhae, a musician of Amon, as well as a head in raw clay and painted stucco. Inserted in the wall of Room 5 is one side of a column from the tomb of Pharaoh Sety I (19th dynasty), removed by Ippolito Rosellini during the expedition to Egypt. Another side of the column, the mirror image of the one in Florence, was removed by Champollion and is now displayed in the Louvre. From the same tomb, discovered by the Italian Giovanni Battista Belzoni in 1817 and considered one of the most beautiful in the Valley of the Kings, comes the bas-relief of the goddess Maat.

Other interesting objects in this room are the large ostrakon *with artists' trials, the faïence plaques of a Ramses foundation deposit and the pink granite statue of the cow goddess Hathor in the act of nursing Pharaoh Horemheb (18th dynasty), coming from the Iseo Campense at Rome.*

Box and ushabti of Tamutnofret

New Kingdom,
XIX-XX dynasties

Plastered and painted wood
Height box 32;
Height *ushabti* 22
Inv. nos. 2187, 2004, 2119, 2121, 2127

The box, divided into two compartments with two lids, is decorated on the longer sides with the image of the deceased Tamutnofret in the act of worshipping the gods Osiris and Anubis, before a table of offerings.

Inside the box are four *ushabti*, the funeral statuettes in the form of mummies destined to work in the fields of the other world in place of the deceased.

19

This fragment of a wall relief contains the upper part of an image of the goddess Maat, personification of the concepts of justice and social order characteristic of Pharaonic society.

On her head is her emblem, a feather, symbol of truth. Engraved round the head of the figure are the words: "Maat, daughter of Ra, the lady who governs the land of silence". The "land of silence" was the necropolis.

The goddess Maat accompanied the souls of the deceased in the other world and presided over the weighing of the heart and judgement before Osiris, god of the dead.

Relief of the goddess Maat

New Kingdom, XIX dynasty
Painted limestone
Height 74
Inv. no. 2469

Room VI

Displayed in Room VI are funerary papyruses, datable from the 18th dynasty to the Ptolemaic Period, containing chapters of the so-called Book of the Dead. *The Egyptian name for the* Book of the Dead *was in reality* Formulas for departure from the day, *and was composed of approximately 190 chapters containing prayers and formulas to show the deceased what was awaiting him after death and how he could overcome the obstacles he would meet in the other world. This room also contains the two Theban sarcophagi of Kent and of Nebtaui, the four canopic jars of Gehuti and stelae of the Heliopolis type in the form of truncated pyramids.*

*Magic papyrus
of Cesmehed(?)khonsu*
(whole and detail)

Third Intermediate Period,
XXI dynasty

Painted papyrus
Lenght 125
Inv. no. 3663

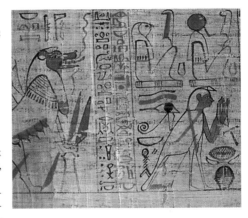

The papyrus presents six painted scenes of deities, daemons and animals. The image of the deceased Cesmedhed(?)khonsu, Amon's musician, appears in the first scene to the right, shown before the god Osiris and a table of offerings. The soul of the deceased is portrayed in the center in the form of a bird with human face. The papyrus, part of a series created for the priests of Amon, contains mythological scenes and magic formulas relevant to the other world rarely found in other funerary texts.

ROOM VII

Room VII is dedicated to material from the 18th and 19th dynasties coming from
the necropolis at Memphis, Saqqara.
Some of the objects displayed here are of exceptional quality, such as the square-
mouthed Faïence goblet (only one other of this shape exists today, in the Louvre),
the relief from the tomb of Ptahmose the priest and the famous Relief with scribes
coming from a wall of the tomb constructed by General Horemheb at Saqqara
before becoming pharaoh and having another tomb cut out of the stone in the
Valley of the Kings.
Among the material displayed in this room are grave goods from the tomb of the
scribe Amenhotep, including a cubit model (showcase 3), a column from the tomb
of Pahemnecer, some commemorative scarabs and numerous wooden or stone
ushabti.
The Statue of the priest Ptahmose probably comes from the temple of Ptah at
Memphis and is a masterpiece from the time of Amenophis III.

*Statue of the priest
Ptahmose*

New Kingdom,
XVIII dynasty

Quartzite
Height 94
Inv. no. 1790

The statue portrays Ptah-
mose, priest of the god
Ptah, crouching on a cu-
shion placed on a paral-
lelepiped base.
Ptahmose has a short wig
with a braid on one side
indicating that he is a
priest.
He wears a fine ankle-
length tunic with a de-
corated apron, and san-
dals on his feet.
The priest is represented
in a position, that of the
so-called cube-statue,
invented at the time of the
Middle Kingdom and wi-
dely diffused in the Late
Period, but rarely used
during the New Kingdom.

Faïence goblet

New Kingdom,
XIX-XX dynasties
Blue faïence
Height 14
Inv. no. 3254

The goblet, of strictly funerary or ritual use, has an elegant shape, with truncated cone foot representing a still half-closed lotus flower whose petals are delineated in low relief on the body of the blue faience vase. The salient characteristic of this rare goblet, made of the enameled material typical of Egypt, is its square mouth. Probably the corners of the lip were intended to indicate the tips of the lotus petals about to open out in flower.

Relief with scribes

New Kingdom,
XVIII dynasty
Limestone
Height 24
Inv. no. 2566

This limestone fragment of a wall relief shows four scribes of the Kingdom intent on their work, writing on tablets.
In their left hands they grasp writing palettes, where the grooves for black and red ink can be seen.
In their right hands they hold the calamus with which they are writing. Note the attempt to represent the figures in perspective.

ROOM VIII

Room VIII conserves the original 19th century decoration planned by Ernesto Schia-
parelli, consisting of a blue sky with stars, walls painted to imitate granite and
wooden showcases in Egyptian style. The room contains material from the Late
Age: funerary stelae, pottery, figured Hellenistic and Roman terra-cottas, and fur-
niture of various kinds including stools, jewel cases, headrests and baskets. The
statuary of the Late Age is represented by some exceptional works: the Statue of
the priest Henat and the bust of a dignitary from Persian times (27th dynasty), da-
ted by the particular type of clothing, a statue of a scribe (fragmentary), and the
capital of a column from Ptolemaic times in the form of the two-faced daemon Bes.
Royal statuary is represented by the bust of a pharaoh (probably Amasi) wearing
the nemès headdress, from the 26th dynasty, and by the gray granite head with the
double crown. Unfortunately the names of both of these statues remain unknown.
The room contains a number of sarcophagi and mummies as well as several sets
of canopic jars, used to hold the organs of the dead extracted during the mum-
mification process.
Of significant interest is the wrapper made of plastered and painted canvas with
gilded decorations which belonged to the girl Takherbed, dating from Ptolemaic
times.

Statue
of the priest Henat

Late Period,
XXVII dynasty

Green basalt
Height 79
Inv. no. 1784

The priest is shown stan-
ding on a base, holding before him a naos on which
is depicted in relief the fa-
cade of the temple of the
goddess Neith at Sais.
The original head of the
statue is missing. The one
we see today was added in
the last century, modeled
on another head found in
this Museum.
The inscriptions engraved
on the statue are a dedi-
cation to Neith and a de-
scription of the respon-
sibilities of Henat, linked
to the cult of this goddess.

*Inner cover
of a priestess'
sarcophagus*

Third Intermediate Period,
XXI-XXII dynasties
Plastered and painted wood
Length 167
Inv. no. 2174

This wooden panel, designed to rest directly over the mummy inside the true sarcophagus, is shaped like a mummified woman.

The deceased, a priestess of Amon whose name remains unknown, wears a wig decorated with ribbons and lotus petals and has a broad usekh collar painted on her chest.

Her arms are crossed over her body, covered by two mirror-image scenes of adoration of deities.

This object comes from the group of sarcophagi and inner covers, preserved in Florence National Archaeological Museum, which were donated by the Egyptian Government to Italy and other European countries.

It was decided to make this donation subsequent to the discovery in 1891 of a storeroom in the Deir el-Bahri locality containing numerous sarcophagi of Theban priests of the god Amon (21st-22nd dynasties).

25

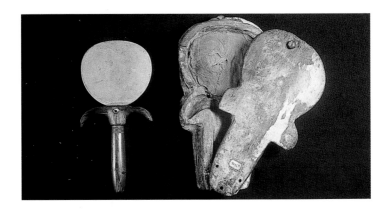

Mirror with case

Late Period,
XXV dynasty

Wood and bronze
Height of mirror 25.5
Inv. no. 3086

The mirror has a gilded bronze disk, slightly flattened in shape, like the sun low on the horizon. The handle is a papyrus-shaped rod, decorated with two wooden pegs and gold-leaf.

The wooden case with cover, in the same shape as the mirror, still conserves its cloth padding.

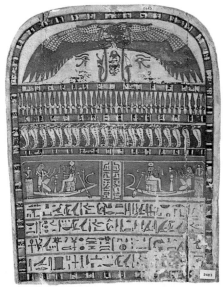

Funerary stele of Taiesimenkheruas

Late Period
Wood and bronze
Height of mirror 35
Inv. no. 2483

On the curved top of the stele is the image of the winged solar disc, surmounting two horizontal decorative friezes.

In the center of the funerary stele are two symmetrical scenes, both depicting the sun boat with the image of the defunct Taisimenkheruas kneeling in adoration of the falcon-headed god Ra, seated on a throne.

Sarcophagus of Cesraperet
(upper part)

Late Period, XXV dynasty

Plastered and painted wood
Length 186.8
Inv. no. 2159

The anthropoid sarcophagus of the defunct Cesraperet, nurse to the daughter of pharaoh Tah-arqa, has a wig decorated with the body of a vulture, symbol of the goddess Mut, wife of Amon. On the breast is painted a broad *usekh* collar under which appears the image of the goddess Nut with outspread wings. The part corresponding to the legs is covered by inscriptions containing prayers taken from funerary texts. The nurse's grave goods consisted of a parallelepiped-shaped sarcophagus containing this inner sarcophagus with the mummy, a wooden funerary stele with gold-leaf decorations and two toilette objects: a *kohl* vase and a mirror with wooden case.

ROOM XI

Room XI contains material dating from the 26th to the 30th dynasty.
One of the most interesting pieces is the so-called Relief of the Arts and Trades *(showcase 2), taken from the wall of an unknown tomb, which shows artisans at work. Objects of interest are the numerous faïence ushabti, all the same, massproduced using moulds in the Late Period, and the faience vases.*
The Sarcophagus of Bakenrenef, *vizier of Pharaoh Psammetico I (26th dynasty) was purchased on the Egyptian antique market by Ippolito Rosellini, but comes from this dignitary's rich tomb in the Saqqara necropolis.*

Sarcophagus of Bakenrenef

Late period,
XXVI dynasty

Limestone
Height 112
Length 220
Width 102
Inv. no. 2182

This sarcophagus belonged to Bakenrenef, vizier to Pharaoh Psammetico I, in the 26th dynasty.
In the shape of a parallelepiped, it is decorated with inscriptions listing the numerous honorific titles of the dignitary and the formulas of dedication to the various deities depicted on the four sides.
On the lid, rounded at the top, is the image of Nut, goddess of the sky, whose open arms are spread wide to protect the sarcophagus and the deceased.

ROOMS XII-XIII

The arrangement of Room XII is temporary. It contains several magic curative stelae representing the god Horus as a child with serpents and crocodiles, datable to the 30th dynasty, as well as various finds from Graeco-Roman times, including numerous ointment jars and glass inlays, and the famous papyrus illustrating the myth of Cupid and Psyche. The two column capitals placed here introduce the visitor to the last room in the Egyptian Museum, dedicated to the Coptic Period and in particular to material coming from the excavations conducted by the Florence Papyrology Institute at the city of Antinous (Middle Egypt).

In addition to objects for everyday use made of bronze, terra-cotta and bone, an ample selection of Coptic fabrics found in the necropolis at Antinous is displayed in a set of drawers. Other interesting items include decorated tunics, socks and caps for children, hair-nets and a silk mantle, which for reasons of conservation are displayed only for brief periods. Among the materials not coming from Antinous are the small limestone heads from decorative high reliefs and the famous papyrus portraying Christ and his Apostles on the Sea of Galilee.

Column capital from Antinous

Coptic Period, 4th-5th century AD
Limestone, height 26
Inv. no. 14496

This capital and its twin surmounted two doorjambs. It is decorated with plant designs and geometric patterns, engraved on the front and inner sides and partially on the rear side, where the block that was inserted in the wall can be seen.

Child's sock

Coptic Period, 4th-5th century AD
Wool, length 14
Inv. no. 12917

The sock, knitted in stripes of different colors and rolled over the instep, has a separate big toe allowing it to be worn with sandals.

Etruscan, Greek and Roman Collections

Etruscan Stone Sculpture *by Anna Rastrelli*

Rooms IX and X on the first floor of Palazzo della Crocetta, which house the Etruscan stone sculpture from the Medicean and Grand Ducal collections, have undergone changes during the successive rearrangements of the museum. For display of the cinerary urns from the Hellenistic Period produced at Chiusi and Volterra, which make up the great majority of the materials in this section, the typological criteria, linked mainly to the subjects displayed in the showcases, has been retained, perpetuating the splitting up of the private collections from which they come, such as those of the Cinci and Galluzzi of Volterra. Room X also contains some statues in full relief, while the three cinerary urns from Chiusi described in this guide form part of the Topographical Museum of Etruria.

Xoanon

Second quarter of the 6th century BC

Pietra fetida, from Chiusi
Height 126
Inv. no. 5506

Throughout the first half of the 6th century BC, *xoana* were produced in Chiusi. These were female busts (over a dozen of them are known), sometimes placed on slender columns composed of elliptical blocks, represented with arms crossed over the breast or grasping their long braids, a gesture of lamentation for the dead.

These statues were designed to be placed outside of the tombs, like the coeval ones of standing male figures cloaked in mantles. The square faces of the "Daedalin" type with wide-open eyes and hair plaited in braids show the influence of Greek sculpture.

Sphinxes
(whole and detail)

First half of the 6th century BC
Pietra fetida,
from Chianciano
Height 78
Length 90
Inv. no. 78716

Statues of real and fantastic animals linked to the Underworld (mainly sphinxes and lions, but also centaurs and sea-horses) were placed outside of the tombs to ward off evil already in the mounds of the orientalizing period. While the former acted as guardians of the tomb, to prevent any profanation of the souls of the deceased, the latter, as hybrids, evoked the horror of the Underworld.

This sphinx, a monster with the body of a winged lion and the head of a woman (the face with its great almond-shaped eyes and braided hair recall that of the coeval *xoana*) is one of the first examples of Chiusi funerary sculpture, highly dependent on that of Vulci.

It is in fact from the southern city that the master workers who launched the Chiusi production seem to have moved, attracted by the availability of *pietra fetida*, a local limestone that owes its name to the foul smell it gives off when abraded.

31

Cinerary urn
from Chiusi

6th century BC

Pietra fetida, from Chiusi
Height 36; length 63;
width 39
Inv. no. 5501
(formerly Servadio Collection)

This small urn, part of a group of monuments decorated in bas-relief from the Archaic Period coming from Chiusi, is decorated on the long sides only with a banquet scene showing two couples lis-

tening to the music of a flute-player and attended by a servant, and with a vivacious dance scene with five figures. On the border are applied small protoms of lions' heads in bronze, reminiscent of the rainspouts on sacred buildings.

The stele is inspired by the figurative experiences of the Greek colonies in the East. The relief sculpture is one of the highest achievements of Chiusi craftsmanship, for its skillful composition and softly modeled but clearly defined relief.

Cippus with musicians

First half of the 5th century BC
Pietra fetida, from Chianciano
Height 55; width 35
Inv. no. 5592

This cippus in the form of a truncated pyramid supported a spherical or onion-shaped crown, now lost. On the lower part are carved four bulls with human heads, while the four sides are decorated with scenes of dancers. This cippus too comes from the archaic Chiusi production decorated in bas-relief.

It is one of the most advanced examples of this production, inspired by Attic pottery painting, in which the quality of the composition is impaired by the repetitive nature of

the scenes. The subjects portrayed on these monuments, like those of the coeval tomb paintings, of which the Chiusi reliefs are reminiscent in style, are for the most part funeral rituals. The diffusion of these monuments (over two hundred are known including cippi, cinerary urns, bases of statues and sarcophagi) shows that in the Archaic Period the self-extolling of the aristocracy was accompanied by the display of an opulent life-style by the more numerous "middle class".

Mater Matuta

Third quarter of the 5th century BC

Pietra fetida, from Chianciano
Height 90; length 58; width 50
Inv. no. 73694

The so-called *Mater Matuta* belongs to the Chiusi production of cinerary statues in *pietra fetida*, where the remains of the deceased were placed in a cavity at the height of the chest, which was then closed by attaching the head, produced separately. This monument, like many others belonging to the same class, was subjected to substantial

additions in the last century, which have now been removed.

It forms part of a group of female figures seated on a throne of oriental type with sphinx-shaped arm rests, which repeat the pattern of the seated male figure having an honorary function in the Middle Archaic Period.

This is the only case in which the woman holds a child in her arms. The generic chthonic attribution of the pomegranate found on many of these monuments is insufficient to identify the figure of the defunct as Persephone, the goddess of Hades. Rather than images of deities, these seem to be women depicted in their opulent splendour of *mater familias*.

The *Mater Matuta* was found in a chamber tomb excavated in the rock with the entrance decorated by two lion cubs, in the Pedata necropolis at Chianciano. Inside the statue, in addition to the ashes of the defunct, were found a small Attic vase representing the head of a woman, a gold pin with the head decorated with gold dust, a gold ring bearing the figure of a warrior and an Etruscan inscription, and two spiral earrings (the ring and earrings have been lost).

Cinerary urn
(whole and detail)
End of the 5ᵗʰ century BC

Pietra fetida, from Chianciano
Height 47; length 120; width 40
Inv. no. 94352

At the end of the 5ᵗʰ century, in Chiusi statuary, the iconography of the deceased portrayed in a semi-reclining position at banquet holding a patera became prevalent, ac-

cording to a model of oriental Greek origin. Subsequently it was enriched with other figures: cupbearers and a female winged daemon seated at the feet of the deceased.
In this example coming from the Pedata necropolis near Chianciano, the best-known monument in the series due to its high quality, the daemon exceptionally holds in his hand

a scroll, symbolizing the written destiny of the defunct. Both figures have separately modeled heads. This monument, more than a cinerary statue, must have been the lid of an urn, like the one described below. The sequence continued into the first decades of the 4ᵗʰ century with workshop pieces of very full and elaborate iconography, although these are often the fruit of 19ᵗʰ century falsifications. The Chiusi cinerary statues from the classic age, which show their dependence on Greek models of Attic tradition filtered through the workmanship of southern Italy, formed a major part of the sculptural production of interior central Etruria, which achieved mature, unified expression at this time.

Cinerary urn from the Bottarone

First half of the 4th century BC

Alabastrine marble,
from the Bottarone locality,
near Città della Pieve
Height 88; length 123;
width 38
Inv. no. 73577

Among the Chiusi cinerary statues from the Classic period, of which this is one of the latest, the Bottarone urn is perhaps the first (if not the only) example in which the woman seated at the feet of the deceased, depicted in the act of lifting the mantle from her head, is undoubtedly his wife. The head of the deceased, reclining at banquet holding a ribbed patera, his right arm resting on his wife's shoulder, had been removed since it was considered false. It has now been recognized as authentic and replaced. Both the clothing of the two figures and the cushions and mattress on the bed have lively polychrome decorations, while the *kline*, decorated by palm leaves, is painted on the chest of the urn.

Although the heads of both figures were carved separately, the monument is a cinerary urn, composed of a lid and a chest. The latter has two cavities to contain two bodies. Beautiful jewelry was found in the urn: necklaces, spiral bindings for the hair, earrings, etc. The figure of the woman was adorned with a gold necklace.

A new material was used for the first time in this monument, alabastrine marble, which during the 3rd century BC superseded *pietra fetida* at Chiusi, used only in the peripheral areas of the territory during the Hellenistic Period.

Cinerary urn from Chiusi (?)

Second half of the 3rd century BC

Alabastrine marble, from Chiusi?
Total height 120; length 91; width 43
Inv. no. 5777

This urn, which comes from the Chiusi production of the Hellenistic Period presenting the deceased at banquet on the lid, has the chest decorated with a mythological scene in high relief: the recognition of Orestes by his sister Iphigenia in Tauris or the Etruscan myth of the diviner Cacu captured by the Vibenna brothers. A poet is portrayed on the shorter sides.

Purni's cinerary urn

Second half of the 3rd century BC

Alabastrine marble, from Città della Pieve
Total height 103; length 82; width 80
Inv. no. 74232

On the front of the chest of this urn, belonging to a member of the Purni family from Chiusi, is a battle scene between Greeks and barbarians, while on the shorter sides are carved a warrior blinded by a bird and one in the act of committing suicide. On the cover is the deceased, banqueting in heroic semi-nudity.

Urn reproducing a building

2nd-1st century BC
Pietra fetida, from Chiusi?
Total height 43.5;
length 51.5; width 34.5
Inv. no. 5539

While the Chiusi urns from the Archaic Period presented architectural structures in the lids shaped like pitched roofs, this one, which reproduces an entire building, is highly important as a documentation of Etruscan architecture. The lid is decorated with a palm tree in the front triangles, while the chest has the form of a one-storey building with a loggia at the top. On the short sides is portrayed an arched door between two columns, on which rest two vases. On the long sides, between two tall columns is a sort of aedicula supported by slender columns. It is impossible to determine whether the building reproduced is a public one or a private dwelling or a tomb generically representing the structure of a house.

Little cinerary urn

Second half of the 2nd century BC
Terra-cotta, from Chiusi?
Height 21; length 35;
width 16
Inv. no. 5692 (lid),
no. 5666 (chest)

This small urn forms part of the Chiusi late production of earthenware cinerary urns produced from moulds, i.e., mass-produced using matrixes and painted in vivid colors. The low cost and the symbolic value of these urns ensured a large-scale production aimed at a class of limited financial possibilities. Depicted on the chest is a hero armed with a plowshaft, long identified as Echetlo, who fought at Marathon.
It has recently been hypothesized that the figure refers to a local myth relevant to the social conflicts that shook Etruria in the 2nd century BC.
On the lid, which is not original, the deceased is portrayed wrapped in a mantle, reclining on a *kline*.

Sarcophagus of
Larthia Seianthi
(whole and detail)

First half of the 2nd century BC
Terra-cotta, from Chiusi
Height 110; length 164
Inv. no. 70978

This sarcophagus with its rich polychrome decorations, the most famous of the limited Chiusi terra-cotta production, was found in the tomb of the Larcna at Chiusi. On the lid the deceased is represented bedecked with jewels, holding a mirror case in her left hand, in the act of lifting the mantle from her face. The chest is decorated by a Doric frieze composed of little columns alternating with ribbed paterae and rosettes, a motif frequently used at Chiusi in the decoration of funerary monuments and architectural elements in terra-cotta. On the upper border is engraved the name of the defunct, Larthia Seianthi, over which a very fragmentary second inscription has been painted in red, showing that the sarcophagus was reutilized. The grave goods included objects in silver and a coin datable between 180 and 189 BC.

Cinerary urn of the family Ceicna Fetiu

First half of the 2ⁿᵈ century BC
Alabaster, from Volterra
Total height 108;
length 88; width 27
Inv. no. 93484

On the lid of the urn the deceased (with head and right arm missing) is portrayed semi-reclining at banquet, no longer with nude torso but wearing a tunic and mantle. On the basis of the inscription (ARNTH FETHIU LARISAL) the urn has been attributed to the powerful Volterra family of the Ceicna Fetiu. On the front of

the chest the scene of the death of Myrtilus is carved in very high relief (the figures are sculpted almost in full relief, like personages moving on a stage framed by two fluted columns). The charioteer, responsible for the death of Enomaos, has taken refuge in a temple, represented by two columns surmounted by urns. He is transfixed with a sword by Pelopes while he seeks refuge beside an altar. Meanwhile Hippodamia tries to tear from his hand the sawed-through wheel of the chariot in which her father has lost his li-

fe, while on the right a priest flees horrified by the sacrilege.

A vase is depicted on the short sides.

This is the eponymous urn of the artisan who produced it, Greek by training if not by origin, known as the Master of Myrtilus, head of the workshop that introduced to Volterra the baroque - style of the Hellenistic kingdoms of Asia Minor, from which derive the colouristic effects, the rich *chiaroscuro* and the dramatic movements unfolding along a few chiastic lines.

39

*Cinerary urn
with Ulysses
and the Sirens*

Second half of the 2nd
century BC
Alabaster, from Volterra
Total height 43; length 69;
width 20
Inv. no. 5782

On the chest of this urn
(produced in a workshop
specialized in subjects
linked to the myth of Ulysses), on which is placed a
non-original lid, appears
the episode of Ulysses and
the Sirens, within the rich
decorative frame typical
of small Volterra urns.
The hero, bound to the
mast of his ship, is listen-
ing to the song of three sirens, portrayed as sump-
tuously dressed women,

like the deceased reclin-
ing on the lid (the myth
was particularly suitable
to women). The sirens,
seated on a reef, are playing the pan-pipe, the ci-
thara and the double flu-
te, a whole orchestra.
The shorter sides of the
urn are undecorated. The
different versions of this
subject, at times very similar to each other, may
have been taken from an
album of cartoons.

*Cinerary urn
from Volterra (?)*

120-110 BC
Alabaster, from Volterra?
Height 30; length 44;
width 18
Inv. no. 5562

On the front of this lidless
urn the voyage of the de-
ceased husband and wi-

fe to the other world is depicted.

The funeral procession, composed of the deceased spouses riding in a *carpentum* (covered chariot) drawn by two mules led by a servant, meets a horseman, shown in the background; behind the chariot walks a man with two children.

The scene is framed above by a serrated motif and below by a Doric frieze composed of tryglyphs alternating with rosettes and ribbed paterae.

The shorter sides of the urn are undecorated.

Subjects linked to the Underworld (departure, voyage to the Other World, apparition of the deceased to his wife, etc.) are typical of the later production of cinerary urns in both Chiusi and Volterra.

Lion

4th-3rd century BC
Nenfro
Height 78; length 138
Inv. no. 5562

This funerary monument portrays a powerful, roaring lion, its tense body stretched forward, its right paw resting on the head of a victim which seems to be a calf but could also be a deer with archaic-style features. The sculpture, which decorated a tomb in the necropolis at the Marta locality near Bolsena, forms part of a series of great stone lions produced starting in the 4th century BC as guardians of tombs, which are among the most impressive Etruscan monuments from this period. This lion seems based not on Greek models but on local taste, recognizable in the stylized mane and muscles, in which echoes of archaism can be detected.

Sarcophagus
of the Amazons
(whole and details)

Third quarter of the 4ᵗʰ
century BC
Insular alabaster,
from Tarquinia
Total height 71;
length 194; width 62
Inv. no. 5811

This sarcophagus, found at Tarquinia in 1869, is one of the most significant and emblematic monuments for the study of ancient painting. Two Etruscan inscriptions executed by different hands, one on the lid and one on the chest, which has damaged the paintings and must therefore have been added later, identify the woman whose remains it held, Ramtha Huzcnai. The pitched lid has four acroterions at the corners, modeled in the shape of female heads, while on the tympanums is sculpted

in bas-relief the myth of Acteon torn to pieces by his hounds between two palm trees sacred to Artemis. The chest is painted in tempera on the four sides with scenes from the myth of the Amazons, in a vast range of colors and surrounded by frames composed of architectural motifs with perspective effects, repeated also on the lid. The figures in the scenes painted on the long sides are distributed in groups according to a repetitive but harmonious pattern, indicative of the artist's strong sense of rhythm: struggles between Amazons riding white horses and Greek hoplites on one side (what must have been the front in ancient times, since one of the inscriptions was carved here) and on the other, two quadrigas bearing Amazons who, crushing

a Greek warrior to the earth, converge with centripetal movement on a group of combatants. On the shorter sides are portrayed a Greek warrior assailed by two Amazons and an Amazon between two Greek hoplites. The first scene and those on the short sides are framed by pillars.

In the mastery of these scenes the high achievements of great Greek painting are obvious. Although the figures are still defined by an outline, relief is suggested by shading and *ombre portate*, while the use of foreshortening suggests a three-dimensional space, especially evident on the short sides.

It is to be hoped that the analysis soon to be conducted on the monument prior to its restoration will identify the cultural am-

*Sarcophagus
of the Amazons*
(details:
left, *shorter side*;
below, *long side with
inscription*)

biance in which it was produced, still subject to debate among scholars. If in fact the chest of the sarcophagus in micro-Asiatic marble, obviously superior to the more mediocre lid, belongs to a type decorated only by painting, for which a Greek or Magna Graecian origin has been hypothesized and if the paintings are inspired by Hellenic megalography of the late 5th century BC, some details are extraneous to the Greek tradition, such as the costumes of the Amazons. It has thus been supposed by some that the sarcophagus was painted by an artist of Greek origin or training who worked at Tarquinia, absorbing local stylistic elements.

ETRUSCAN BRONZES *by Antonella Romualdi*

*The Florence Archaeological Museum possesses the most important collection of
Etruscan bronzes in Italy. It consists of large bronze statues from the Medicean Collection (Chimera, The Haranguer) and small bronzes coming from the Medicean
and Grand Ducal Collections. In the 19ᵗʰ century the Archaeological Museum also
received material from important votive sites in northern Etruria*

Chimera

(whole and detail)

Late 5ᵗʰ-early 4ᵗʰ century BC
Hollow bronze
Height 78,5; length 129
Inv. no. 1

This statue was discovered in 1553 outside the walls of Arezzo in the vicinity of Porta San Lorentino during excavation for the construction of new fortifications. Cosimo I de' Medici, reports Vasari, ordered that this magnificent sculpture be brought to Florence at once. The discovery of the *Chimera* assumed great significance for Cosimo I since it became the symbol of Medici power representing the wild beasts that the Duke had overcome to build his reign.

In accordance with the decorative scheme of the Medici residence, the *Chimera* was placed in the Hall of Leo X in Palazzo Vecchio, from which only in 1718 was it transferred to the southern Corridor of the Uffizi along with other great bronzes from the Medicean collections. Since 1870 it has been a part of the Florence Archaeological Museum Collections. The paws on the left side have been crudely restored utilizing lead castings. A tradition, now considered fallacious, attributed the restoration to Benvenuto Cellini. The tail in the form of a serpent biting one of the horns of the goat's head, a variation not found in ancient iconography, is the work of the sculptor Francesco Carradori, who executed it in 1785 as replacement for the original one which, not having been salvaged at the time of the

44

discovery, was never attached.

The bronze statue represents the unsubdued beast at the moment of its final encounter with the Corinthian hero Bellerophon, when already deadly wounded, as shown by the goat's head bleeding and drooping to one side, it is about to launch a last desperate attack, crouching back to strengthen its bound and unleashing all of its savage energy to terrify its adversary. The tension of the body with its taut muscles and nerves portrayed in their tremendous force is admirably shown by the artisan.

The mane bristling in pointed locks, along with the eyes (new lost) and the fangs executed separately in a different metal and then inserted emphasized still further the terrible strength of the beast which was to be conquered by the hero with the aid of Pegasus, the winged horse given him by Athena or Poseidon.

The *tinscvil* inscription, engraved before casting, which appears on the right front paw, in a graphic form typical of the Val di Chiana area (Cortona, Arezzo), identifies the *Chimera* as a monumental votive gift offered to the goddess Tinia. This text appears again on so-

me small bronze votive statuettes found at Cortona and on altars dedicated to the cult of Tinia found at Volsinii Orvieto). While the iconography and style can be compared with Attic red-figured vases and with a bronze support possessed by the Florence Archaeological Museum (Inv. no.

674), showing reflections from the Magna Graecia milieu, the place where the statue was produced is still hotly debated.

Today it seems highly probable that it was created in Arezzo or in any case in the Val di Chiana, with the aid of artisans from Orvieto.

The Haranguer
(whole and detail on next page)

Early 1th century BC or first half of the 2nd century BC

Hollow bronze: seven different parts (head with neck, trunk in two pieces, right arm, left hand and legs) later assembled together
Height 179
Inv. no. 2

The statue, received by Cosimo I de' Medici – according to Vasari – in September 1566, was found by chance by a peasant at Pila near Perugia in the

while the right arm is lifted high, the fingers spread slightly apart in a gesture commonly interpreted as that of *silentium manu facere* before beginning a public oration.

A dedicatory inscription is engraved on the lower border of the toga, consisting of twelve words distributed over three lines: *AULESI METELIS VE(LUS) VESIAL CLENSI/CEN FLERES TECE SANSL TENINE/ TUTHINES CHISVLICS*, in favor of Aule Meteli son of Vei and of a Vesi to the god Tece Sans, in whose sanctuary the statue, depicting an influential member of the ruling class of a Roman town, presumably Perugia, was erected in about 80 BC by a community not clearly identified.

A recent hypothesis, formulated on the basis of comparisons with painted tombs and carvings on sarcophagi and urns from the late 2nd-3rd centuries BC and on the costume of *The Haranguer* as well as the stylistic characteristics of the portrait, interprets the gesture as the expression of a prayer dictated by *pietas* toward the gods, suggesting dating in the first half of the 2nd century BC. This hypothesis is further confirmed by the paleography of the inscription.

Papal State, from where it was stealthily and adventurously transported to Florence.

According to the tradition reported in 1591 by a representative of the Grand Ducal government at Cortona, *The Haranguer* came from a sanctuary in the Sanguinara locality on Lake Trasimeno. *The Haranguer* remained in the room of Cosimo I in Palazzo Pitti up to 1588, when it was included in the Gallery of statues that was

to form the first core of the Uffizi.

The statue portrays a male personage in the fullness of maturity, characterized by a face which is severe but simultaneously grave and inspired. He wears a short toga (*exigua*) with decorated border (*praetexta*), above a tunic with an angustus clavus (a vertical stripe along the side); his footwear is of the type known as "senatorial". On his left hand he wears a ring,

Head of a young man

c. 330 BC
Hollow bronze
Height 23
Inv. no. 548

The head belonged to a life-size votive statue portraying a young man with highly idealized features. The solidity of the bone structure, the soft modeling of the face, the particular rendering of the hair and the thick eyebrows, the eyes with inserted irises made of another material, and the clearly marked full-lipped mouth show the high artistic level achieved by Etruscan bronze-making workshops, and call to mind a head found at Fiesole, now in the Louvre Museum of Paris.
Considered a cornerstone of the portrait tradition defined "Middle Italic", that is, characteristic of the sculpture of central Italy up to the beginning of the 2nd century BC, the head appears well rooted within the ambience of a series of youthful heads documented all over Etruria in both painting and sculpture, in votive figures and in pottery.

Statue of Minerva

Roman copy (early 1st century AD) of a Greek original from 340-330 BC

Hollow bronze
Height 155
Inv. no. 3

Found by chance at Arezzo (1541) while a well was being dug near the Church of San Lorenzo, the statue became part of the furnishings of the *scrittoio* of Cosimo I in 1559. Exhibited in the Uffizi (southern Corridor) in 1789, it was transferred to the Florence Archeological Museum in 1890. A variation created in the early Imperial Period of a type of Athena called Vescovali –from a statue in the collection of the same name now at St. Petersburg–the Arezzo Minerva has been subjected to heavy restoration, clearly visible in the lower part. The right arm, previously executed in plaster, was restored in bronze by Francesco Carradori in 1785.

Bibbona goat

Late 6th-early 5th century BC

Solid bronze
Height 22; length 26;
weight 1.480 kg
Inv. no. 70792

Part of a votive offering consisting of 52 Etruscan bronzes (idols, warriors and animals), almost none of which can now be identified in the collection of small bronzes purchased for the Uffizi for the amount of 300 Lire, the goat was found in 1868 below the castle of Bibbona (Province of Livorno), six miles from the sea. The animal is portrayed at a moment of highest tension, leaping into a run to flee a predator, a victim of the terror that drives it to turn it head violently backward.

A work of extraordinary quality, it must have formed part of the decorations applied to the lip or shoulder of a vase of exceptional worth, probably produced in one of the bronze-workers shops of Populonia.

Group of bronze statuettes of women from the votive offerings of the Fonte Veneziana in Arezzo

c. 530- 500 BC

Solid bronze
Height from 6.5 to 9.5
Inv. nos. 256, 234, 228,
266, 264,263,267,258

Images of the devout offered to a deity were found at Arezzo in 1869 in a group of votive offerings from a suburban sanctuary linked to the cult of waters, which originally included 180 bronze idols, gold and silver rings, buccheri, and a great quantity of raw metal (*aes rude*).

All produced by the same Arezzo workshop strongly influenced by Ionic sculpture, they reiterate the type of the standing *kore* with *tutulus* and *calcei*, lifting the hem of a richly decorated garment with her left hand.

49

Priest

Early 5th century BC
Solid bronze
Height 27.5
Inv. no. 72725

This statuette, found by chance in 1883 by a wood-gatherer on Isola di Fano (near Fossombrone), on the right bank of the Taru-go, can be traced to the group of votive offerings linked to the cult of waters, already discovered in 1875, which contained another 6 statuettes of Umbrian type in addition to armillae, bronze paterae and fragments of pottery. It is a product of very high quality produced by a bronze-working shop located in interior northern Etruria. Identification of the personage is still uncertain, being variously interpreted by experts as a deity, a high-ranking personage, a priest or a haruspex.

The garments worn by the figure are extremely interesting: the cap, similar to the petasus of Turms or of Menrva, resembling that of the haruspex, the characteristic wand held in the left hand, and the snake-shaped ribbon applied to the left shoulder, which was then to become typical of female personages of high rank in the Classic and Hellenistic periods.

Statuette of the god Laran

Mid-5th century BC
Solid bronze
Height 5.3. Inv. no. 586

The statuette represents a warrior advancing in battle. With extended left arm bent at the elbow he holds a shield before him, while with his right arm drawn slightly back and raised he grasps a lance, now lost. He wears a helmet of Attic type with decorated front and a breastplate over a light tunic leaving the genitals bare. On his legs are richly decorated shin-guards. The face with its strongly marked features is well modeled, with large eyes and clearly outlined lips. This is a refined work of high quality probably produced in a town located in interior Etruria (Chiusi or Orvieto), within the context of a culture that embraced the entire area traversed by the Tiber, as far as Arezzo, in the Classic Period. In the 19th and 20th centuries various imitations or replicas of this bronze statuette were made, one of which is now in the British Museum at London.

Javelin thrower

540-530 BC
Solid bronze
Height 7
Inv. no. 91379

The statuette has been recognized as coming from the Bibbona votive offerings, which also included the Goat, found in 1868 and subsequently transferred from the Uffizi Gallery to the Florence Archaeological Museum. It is one of the oldest examples of the representation of a javelin thrower.

The javelin rod, now missing, was curved and bent forward, perhaps in modern times. It ended in a cylindrical part and a characteristic narrowing. The body, still rather stiff, appears well modeled in the lower part.

Hercules at rest

Late 4th-early 3rd century BC
Solid bronze
Height 28
Inv. no. 5

The statuette, which portrayed Hercules standing in a position of repose, his weight on the right leg, the left slightly advanced and bent at the knee, comes from Poggio Castiglione (Massa Marittima), where a defensive settlement linked to Vetulonia has been identified.

The hero wears the *leonté* (lionskin), one of his characteristic attributes along with the club.

The lion's face serves as a hood over his head, its front legs are tied over his chest while the rest of the skin, its thick, upstanding mane portrayed with great refine-

ment, lies over the left arm like a mantle. The hero seems about to make an offer to the chthonic deities.

He holds a piece of fruit, perhaps a pomegranate, in his left hand, a drinking horn in his right.

The pose is strongly influenced by the formal schemes derived from the work of the Greek sculptor Praxyteles.

*Bronze kitchenware
and furnishings*
4th-5th century BC

In the third showcase are
numerous bronze objects
found at Talamone in

1877, during excavations
conducted by the Vivarelli
family in a necropolis situated on their land. There
are vases used for banqueting such as the egg-shaped situla, paterae,
and pitchers, of which numerous handles with carved decoration at the bottom are conserved; bowls,
and objects used to dip or
filter wine (such as the
kyathoi or single-handled vases with body in the
form of a distaff, and the
strainers visible on the
lower shelf).

Among the most interesting objects are the patera with handle in the
form of Lasa, attributable to a Vulci workshop,
and the vase shaped like
a woman's head.

*Mirror with Hercules
and Uni*

Mid-4th century BC
Cast bronze with engraved
decoration
Length 31; diameter 19
Inv. no. 72740

This mirror, with cast handle and quadrangular
plate with flared margins,
and disc decorated by a
crown of beads in relief,
comes from Volterra and
was purchased by the Museum in 1884. The scene
engraved on the back is
highly interesting. In the
center against a background of two fluted

columns with Aeolian capitals the goddess Uni, seated on a throne, her feet resting on a footstool, lifts her mantle with her right hand while with her left she offers her breast to Hercules who, bearded and wearing the *leonté*, leans on his club as he bends toward her. Behind them are two half-hidden female figures, one of whom may be Turan.

To the left of Hercules the god Aplu is portrayed standing, wearing a crown and a mantle and bearing a laurel branch in his right hand. To the left of Uni stands Tinia, viewed from the left profile. In her left hand she carries a long scepter while her right arm, bent upward, holds a quadrangular table on which is engraved an Etruscan inscription of five lines, which seems almost an explanatory caption to the scene.

Within the bands surrounding the main scene a Silenus holding a patera in his right hand is depicted at the top while an Eros with a bulla around his neck and an egg in his right hand appears at the bottom.

These accessory figures in particular seem to suggest Orphism. The myth, of Greek origin, is referred to on two other ancient mirrors only.

Mirror with Laran and Celsclan

Mid-5th century BC

Cast bronze with engraved decoration
Length 20.8;
diameter 16.3
Inv. no. 79283

The mirror, furnished with a forked appendix for inserting the bone handle, comes from Populonia.

On the back, within a frame formed of a branch of ivy resting on a base of two scrolls, is a scene of combat between two warriors, identified by the inscriptions as Laran, the Etruscan god of war, and the son of Cel, an Etruscan deity perhaps akin to Ghe – the Earth – as

mother goddess, whose name appears on five statuettes of offerers found in a votive offering near Lake Trasimeno.

Laran is portrayed about to strike his enemy with a sword. His adversary, bareheaded, long hair flying in the wind, flees to the right, turning backward and lifting a millstone to hurl at the god of war.

The pattern of two warriors facing each other with legs crossed at the center of the scene was widely used in the production of figured mirrors datable to the mid-5th century BC.

GRAECO-ROMAN BRONZES *by Anna Rastrelli*

Most of the large and small Greek and Roman bronzes transferred to the Archaeological Museum from the Uffizi in 1890, within the context of restructuring of the Florentine Museums, originally formed part of the Medicean and Grand Ducal Collections. The great Horses' head *belonged to Lorenzo the Magnificent,* The Livorno Torso *and the portrait* Bust of Antinous *were among the collections of Cosimo I, while the so-called* Idolino of Pesaro *arrived at Florence from Pesaro as a wedding gift for Grand Duke Ferdinando II in 1630.*

Unfortunately, only a few of the large bronze statues from antiquity have come down to us. Starting in the early Middle Ages they were frequently melted down due to the scarcity of metals; occasionally a pale echo of them can be glimpsed in some of the small bronzes.

Medici-Riccardi horse's head

Mid-4th century BC
Bronze, height 83
Inv. no. 1639

This horse's head, whose provenance as well as the circumstances in which it was found are unknown, must have formed part of a life-size equestrian statue. The working technique and the metal alloy employed seem to support the hypothesis that it is an original Greek statue, dating between the late Classic and the early Hellenistic Period. This is confirmed by the fact that the gold-leaf gilding, which had suggested that it was a Roman replica, was applied to the statue at a later time over layers of corrosion that had already stabilized. The statue formed part of the collection of Lorenzo the Magnificent and was placed in the garden of Palazzo Medici-Riccardi, from which, after the expulsion of the Medici family, it was transferred to Palazzo Vecchio. At the return of the Medici it was restored by Bartolomeo Cennini and brought back to the garden of the palace in Via Larga, where it was used as the mouth of a fountain.

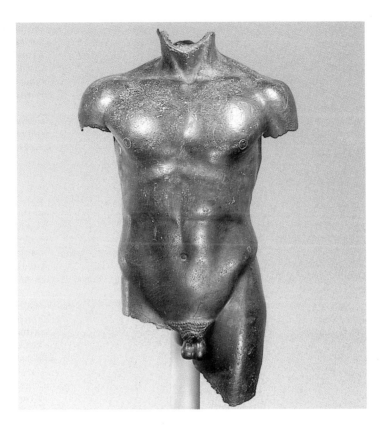

Livorno Torso

From a Greek original
of the 5th century BC

Bronze
Height 92
Inv. no. 1638

Due to its missing parts
it is impossible to iden-
tify the subject of this
statue portraying a young
standing nude as deity,
hero, or victorious athlete. The news that it came
from Livorno, reported
only in 1860, is not backed
up by information from
any archives, although
analysis of the encrus-
tations on the inner sur-
face of the bronze show
that it was salvaged from
the sea. The dating of the
Livorno Torso, which
must have belonged to
the collection of Cosimo
I, is still debatable.
While some scholars con-
sider it to be a Roman
copy of a Greek original,
of which however no
other replicas are known,
others believe it to be an
original Greek work, da-
ted variously during the
first half of the 5th century BC, and attributed to
different schools of art:
from Attic, to Oriental
Greek, to Italic Ionic.

relief, one portraying the sacrifice of a goat to Dionysus, the other the *Triumph of Ariadne*.

In July 1630 Duke Francesco Maria della Rovere, having no other heirs, sent the Idolino to Florence as a gift for his niece Vittoria, engaged to Ferdinando II, Grand Duke of Tuscany.

Initially placed in the Florence Armeria and then in the Uffizi Gallery, the *Idolino* was moved to the Florence Archaeological Museum at the turn of the century.

The statue portrays a nude

Idolino of Pesaro
(whole and details)

1st century AD

Bronze
Height 149
Inv. no. 1637

Found in October 1530 at Pesaro and immediately donated to the Duke of Urbino Francesco Maria della Rovere, the ancient bronze statue of the so-called *Idolino* was restored in the following decade.

The splendid Renaissance bronze base, attributed to Girolamo Lombardo, was created prior to 1535. On the front it bears an inscription composed by Cardinal Pietro Bembo and on the sides two plaques decorated in bas-

56

youth, holding in his left hand a great vine-shoot with clusters of grapes (detached already in 1656; a fragment of it is now in the Bargello National Museum), which had initially caused it to be identified as Bacchus. In the left hand he holds what seems to be a small table, attributes that classify the Idolino as a decorative or functional sculpture.

It may in fact be a *trapezophoros*, a table holder, or a lamp carrier to illuminate the nocturnal banquets held in the *domus* of the prominent family to which it belonged.

Since the time of its finding the statue was considered an original Greek work of high artistic level, deemed even by Winckelmann to be one of the most beautiful sculptures come down to us from ancient Greece.

As such it enjoyed great fame, becoming a model for artists.

In reality the statue is a classicizing re-elaboration from the Augustan period of a Polycletean original of eclectic invention datable to the end of the Hellenistic age.

Portrait bust of Antinous
2ⁿᵈ century AD

Bronze; height 30.5
Inv. no. 1640

This portrait, which formed part of the collection of Cosimo I, is one of the many portrayals of the youth who was the Emperor Hadrian's favorite, who died of drowning in the Nile in 130 AD and was honored as a divinity in numerous parts of the Empire. This head, along with eighty or so replicas, can be traced back to a single original produced in Athens immediately after the death of the young man. In the past considered a Renaissance copy, it is recognized today as an ancient original, the only one in bronze that has come down to us.

Portrait bust of Homer

Late 16ᵗʰ - early 17ᵗʰ century AD
Bronze, from Meloria
Height 43
Inv. no. 1646

This portrait bust was found in 1722 in the waters of Meloria off the coast of Livorno, along with another three (of Aeschylus, Sophocles and a still unidentified personage). Deemed ancient by most of the experts and considered to be bronze replicas from the Flavian period of Greek originals of different epochs, the busts have recently been identified as Renaissance reproductions of Roman copies, of which they repeat even the modern restoration.

Zeus

1st–2nd century AD

Bronze; height 29.7
Inv. no. 2291

The almost total disappearance of the large Greek bronzes represents a loss that can only in part be compensated for by Roman copies in marble and by bronze replicas. Although these statuettes are small, they nonetheless transmit an image of the masterpieces from they were derived. This bronze statuette portraying Zeus with the thunderbolt (the left arm bearing the mantle was executed separately) has in fact been linked to originals by Phydias or Myron.

Amazon

2nd century AD
Bronze
Height 24.4
Inv. no. 2293

This bronze statuette, known since the early 18th century, although impoverished by its small size and by the Late Renaissance restoration (the arms are modern: the right hand originally rested on the head), hands down to us an image of one of antiquity's most famous statues: the *Wounded Amazon* sculpted by Polycletus in competition with Phydias, Cresila and Phradmon and dedicated in the sanctuary of Ephesus between 440 and 430 BC. This *Amazon* may belong to the series of replicas known as the "Sciarra type".

Jason

3rd century BC-16th century AD
Bronze
Height 44.5
Inv. no. 547

Not infrequently a Renaissance artist decided to complete an ancient fragment of sculpture, transforming it according to modern taste, often with happy results. This is the case of the so-called *Jason*: a bronze statuette of a winged cherub, perhaps an Eros, of Etruscan production holding a vase now lost, which must originally have decorated a lamp, has been combined with a youthful figure that bears him on his shoulders. The statuette is attributed to the Renaissance sculptor Pietro Angeli da Barga.

POTTERY WITH GEOMETRIC DECORATIONS *by Anna Maria Esposito*

This collection is practically unique in Italy insofar as it contains materials from factories not documented up to now by excavations conducted in our country. Formerly incorporated in the section of the Museum dedicated to "Pre-Hellenistic and Proto-Greek Antiquities" which, according to its director Luigi Adriano Milani was supposed to furnish terms of comparison for Etruscan products, this pottery comes from collections of various formation: a donation from the Athens National Museum to which was given in exchange Etruscan material, in the early 20th century; donations from L. A. Milani himself and from Georg Karo (a German archaeologist born in Italy, raised in Florence and for several years director of the Athens section of the Germanic Archaeological Institute); and lastly purchased by the Museum.

Pyxis with geometric decoration
(whole and detail)
760-750 BC

Pottery, Filla Group
Height 20
Inv. no. 84807

In the 9th and 8th centuries BC pottery characterized by predominantly geometric decorations, rendered with strict precision (straight, angular, compass motifs) was produced especially in Attica. The repertoire of shapes, many of which were no longer produced after this period, was extremely varied (amphorae, craters, jugs, goblets, pyxises). This is the case of the cylindrical pyxis, typical of Attic production and found in both male and female tombs as container for objects of various kinds. The painted geometric decoration is enriched on the lid by a sculptured group of three small horses, which may allude to the team of a racing chariot consisting of two horses harnessed to the shaft plus one for reinforcement. The presence of holes on the lip and edge seem to indicate that these vases were suspended by cords.

Amphora

First half of the 8th century BC
Pottery
Height 50
Inv. no. 4310

Found mainly in tombs, vases decorated with geometric figures were destined to accompany the deceased in his last voyage or to contain his ashes.
Characteristic of women's tombs is the amphora with handles placed on the neck and shoulder, like this elegant example of Attic production from the Middle Geometric II period (800-760 BC).
The tall slender neck is decorated by a labyrinth, a motif very widely used in all Greek art, which at this time reached its traditional formulation.

Funerary amphora from Boeotia

700-690 BC
Pottery
Height 66
Inv. no. 4283

The most monumental vases were placed on tombs as true funerary emblems.
This great amphora has a high flared neck and broad egg-shaped body with rod-like handles.
The decorative scheme, strictly limited to linear patterns, repeats the usual motif of the meander, here continuous and filled in with shading, covering two ample areas on the shoulder between the handles. The neck is vertically striped with groups of zig-zag motifs.

The amphora comes from a typical production of Boeotia, the region bordering on Attica, but similar vases have also been found in necropolises on the Cyclades islands.

63

ATTIC POTTERY *by Anna Maria Esposito*

The curators of the Medici and Lorraine collections were less interested in the art of drawing in antiquity, as exemplified on painted pottery, than in other subjects, bronze statuary for instance. Nonetheless the Florentine Galleries collected important groups of figured vases, particularly in the 18th and 19th centuries. Throughout the 18th century these vases, found in great quantity in the necropolises of ancient Italy, were universally considered to be of Etruscan make. Luigi Lanzi, curator of the Grand Ducal collections from 1775, in developing one of Winckelmann's intuitive guesses, demonstrated the Greek matrix of the figured vases on the basis of the myths represented and the inscriptions in the Greek language and alphabet. From the information furnished by Lanzi it can be assumed that still at the end of the 18th century Greek figured vases were represented by a rather small number of examples, coming from both the Medicean Collections (Lorenzo and Cosimo I) and private bequests. Under the Lorraines, thanks to the work of Lanzi, who had become supervisor of Pietro Leopoldo's Gabinetto delle Terre, the collection was first substantially enlarged by the acquisition of vases found in the lands of the Grand Duchy (Volterra, Montepulciano, Valdichiana). The great season of excavations in the first half of the 19th century, involving the main Etruscan necropolises, enriched the Florentine Galleries with significant core collections: in 1830 an ex-

traordinary group of figured vases from the Classical Period coming from the Tuscan Maremma, later the exceptional krater known as the "François Vase" discovered at Chiusi in 1844-45 by the archaeologist Alessandro François, and the group coming from the excavations conducted by the Colombaria Society at Roselle, Sovana and Chiusi from 1858 to 1861. After the decree establishing the Egyptian-Etruscan Museum became effective on March 17, 1870, the pottery from the Grand Ducal Collections was transferred from the Uffizi Gallery to the Cenacolo del Foligno in Via Faenza, site of the new Museum. To this already substantial core was added, at the initiative of Gianfrancesco Gamurrini, Conservator of Antiquities, a large part of the exceptional collection of Marchese Campana, which, piled up in the storerooms of the Monte di Pietà pawnbrokers in Rome after his bankruptcy, was dispersed in collections and museums throughout Europe and the world. Lastly, the collections were further enriched through the dedicated work of L. A. Milani, first director of the Royal Archaeological Museum, opened in Palazzo della Crocetta "almost in silence" in 1881. After the creation of the Topographical Museum of Etruria which was to house from then on all of the materials coming from excavations, all of these collections were reunited in the Antiquarium, subsequently to be incremented only through purchases and donations.

KLEITIAS AND ERGOTIMOS
"François Vase". Black-figured Attic krater
(*Side A*, on the preceding page;
Handle with "Achilles and Ajax",
detail on the right;
Side B, on the next page)

570 BC

Pottery; height 66
Inv. no. 4209

Discovered at Dolciano, near Chiusi, around 1844-1845, the great black-figured krater of Athenian production, known as the "*François Vase*" from the name of the archeologist Alessandro François, has remained in Italian public collections only due to the lucky circumstance of having been found on a farm belonging to the Grand Duke. A true masterpiece of the potter's art, the krater, created in about 570 BC, is unique in its shape, inspired by metal models, its size and its remarkable composition. The two artisans, Kleitias the painter and Ergotimos the potter, who signed their names on the vase twice, must have been well aware of its exceptional quality. The very rich decoration is distributed over the surface of the vase in overlapping bands, where the narrative unfolds with incomparable detail and clarity in an extraordinary crowd of personages, each accompanied by an inscription indicating the name. On the shoulder of the vase the solemn procession of deities celebrating the marriage of Peleus and Thetis winds on incessantly. The gods, dressed in sump-

65

tuous colorful garments, each marked by his name and characteristic attributes, proceed in couples, riding in majestic quadrigas drawn by black and white horses or walking, in groups like the three Cariti or alone like the smiling Dionysus who bears a great amphora on his shoulders. Leading the procession is the centaur Chiron, a creature of the wild who was then to become the wise tutor of the child Achilles. On the threshold of his palace of Phthias, Peleus receives his guests with a gesture of greeting while Thetis, his bride, waits modestly half-concealed within the house. The lower frieze, on the front of the vase, narrates an episode from the Trojan war, that of the trap laid by Achilles' for Troilus, the young son of Priam, surprised by the Greek hero while drawing water from a fountain with his sister Polissena. The frightened girl flees, dropping the typical three-handled pitcher used for water, the name of which is indicated: *hydria*. On the back the episode of Hephaestus' return to Olympus accompanied by Dionysus and Silenus, who carries a wineskin, is depicted. The lip and neck of the krater are decorated with the mythological Caledonian wild boar hunt conducted by Peleus and Meleager, the funeral games in honor of Patroclus, the Greek hero and friend of Achilles, the return to Crete of Theseus' ship with the joyful dance of the young boys and girls saved from the Minotaur by the hero, and the struggle between Lapiths and Centaurs. The battle between the Pygmies and the cranes which concludes the sequence of stories on the foot of the vase has been justly compared, for its "comic" subject, to the satiric drama that followed a tragic sequence. Lastly, on the handles, are Artemis, represented as lady of the animals and, in the space below, Ajax bearing the body of Achilles.

SAKONIDES
Black-figured lip-cup

mid-6th century BC
Pottery; height 10
Inv. no. 71009

Starting in the mid-6th century BC a group of artisans called "Minor Masters" for the "miniaturistic" taste of their painting dedicated themselves to the decoration of small, refined vases, tall-stemmed goblets in particular. Due to the frequent custom of signing the vases by the artisan's name followed by the verbs *epoiesen* (made) or *egrapsen* (painted), we know not only the names but also the specializations of many of these potters and painters. Sakonides, a pottery painter, signed under the handle this small and luminous *lip-cup* (cup with a distinct, separate lip) coming from Pescia Romana.

The decoration, the head of a woman on the border of the lip and little polychrome palms along the handles, provides an elegant complement to the shape, accompanying and emphasizing its lines.

NICOSTHÉNES
Eye cup

530-520 BC
Pottery; height 12
Inv. no. 3888

Nicosthénes, potter and proprietor of a workshop active between 540 and 520 BC, worked almost exclusively for the Etruscan market.
Experimenting with new and original solutions for the more usual vase shapes, such as the cup, and highly attentive to the demands of the customers, he transposed shapes typical of the Etruscan bucchero into the language of Attic black figures.
From the shop of Nikosthénes come various examples of "eye-cup".
Between two great stylized eyes, obviously the simplified image of a face or a Gorgon's mask, appears the figured scene: either a simple figure or a small group.
The formula "Nikosthénes *epoiesen*" (Nikosthénes made it), painted very clearly, accompanies the sinuous contour of the eye on this cup, datable around 540 BC, with a scene of lions and panthers savagely attacking a deer.

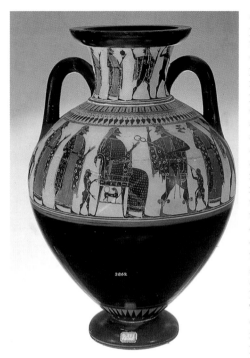

MANNERED PAINTER
Amphora
with separate neck

540-530 BC
Pottery; height 45
Inv. no. 3862

Between 550 and 520 BC a curious potter, called the Mannered Painter for the stiff, highly mannered style of his work, was active in Ceramics, the potters' quarter in Athens. Dedicating himself in particular to the decoration of monumental amphorae, often of unusual shape, the Mannered Painter took the taste for decoration to extreme consequences in compositions rich in detail but almost entirely devoid of narrative content. This painter's favorite shape was the ovoid amphora, in a wide range of variations: from the most common type, with echinus-shaped mouth and foot, rod-like handles and decoration unfolding in a continuous frieze, to the most peculiar type with rounded mouth, large jointed foot and ribbon handles in which the figured scene occupies only the central part of the frieze, while the area under the handles is filled with an ample and elaborate inflorescence. This amphora presents a continuous decoration on the neck and shoulder. A scene of courtship in which a cloaked and bearded figure offers a gift to a youth, among figures who seem to have no direct relationship with the main group, is depicted in the limited space of the neck, while the wide curve of the shoulder contains the imposing images of the enthroned Zeus and Hermes among cloaked figures.

The taste for design and decoration is very evident in the abundance of overpainted parts and filling details: white rosettes and red dots embellish the sumptuous garments, a little panther decorates Zeus' throne whose back ends in a swan's head, two small human figures and a bird in flight fill the spaces between the personages.

This exuberant decoration is unable to conceal the painter's distinguishing traits, to which he owes his name – the wooden stiffness of the images, the affectation of the gestures, and the absence of any consistent narrative framework.

BERLIN PAINTER
Red-figured pelìke

510-500 BC
Pottery
Height 34
Inv. no. 3985

Around 530 BC a fundamental change occurred in Attic pottery painting, with the adoption of a new technique that was to alter the very concept of vase painting: this was the red-figured technique. The figures were no longer filled in with black, but left in red on the painted background of the vase, and the details were no longer engraved but painted. This innovation, which allowed greater freedom and suppleness in drawing, soon superseded the customary black-figured technique which, still used by painters of little artistic worth, was later definitively abandoned. In the late 6th and early 5th centuries BC the shops in the Athens Ceramics district followed certain precise production trends, and pottery painters specialized in decorating large vases or goblets.

Among the pottery painters dedicated to the decoration of large red-figured vases the Berlin Painter, who owes his name to an amphora now in Berlin, occupies a position of unrivaled supremacy as one of the highest personalities in the history of Athenian vase painting.

This *pelìke* illustrating two of the feats of Theseus, the struggle with the Minotaur and the encounter with Sinis, is attributed to the artists' early years.

The compositions are forceful and dramatic, especially the scene of the slaying of the Minotaur. The group among which stands Theseus, driving his sword into the belly of the monster who sinks lifeless as a red gush of blood spurts from his wound (the true visual center of the composition) is framed, according to archaic usage, by the figures of three youths who emphasize the drama of the event through vigourous gesticulation. What were to become the special characteristics of the painter's mode of "narrating by images" are already declared here: no longer a myth or episode depicted as it takes place, but summarized and fixed in its crucial moment, according to the suggestions of contemporary theater.

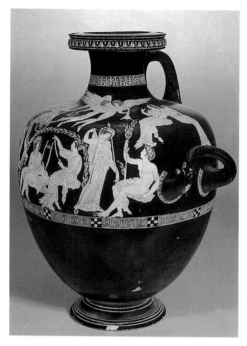

MEIDIAS PAINTER
Red-figured hydria

450 BC
Pottery
Height 46
Inv. no. 81947

In the last decade of the 5th century BC the crisis of values linked to political instability and the uncertain outcome of the war with Sparta led, in the figurative arts, to a break with classical equilibrium and the formation of an elegant, mannered language, defined "florid style".

The works of the Meidias Painter (420-400 BC) are fully expressive of formal elegance and decorative abundance. To him is attributed this precious *hydria* which, along with its "twin" and a fine group of bronze grave goods, were found at Populonia in the tomb of a woman of high rank.

The perfect harmony of the painted surfaces is obvious on both the rear, finely decorated with elegant inflorescence, and the front where complex, elegant scenes unfold.

In an idyllic, rarefied atmosphere, Phaon softly plays the lyre for Demonassa, while Aphrodite, the goddess of love, who has transformed the old boatman Phaon into a youth loved by all women, rises swiftly on a chariot drawn by *Himeros* (the "desire for love") and *Pòthos* (the "lament of love"). Protagonist of the artist's serene, joyful world is the goddess of love accompanied by elegantly dressed and bejeweled girls who represent abstract concepts or states of mind (*Eutychìa*, "good luck"; *Eudaimonìa*, "happiness"), identifiable through their painted names (no longer clearly legible).

The opulence of the scene is emphasized by the overpainting, but above all by real gilding using gold-leaf for the wings of the cupids and the jewels of the girls and the goddesses.

The choice of pleasant, reassuring subjects seems almost a reaction to the uncertainty and difficulty of a historical moment marked by the long war with Sparta which, concluding in the defeat of Athens, was to lead progressively to a crisis in the *polis* and to the end of democracy.

GRAECO-ROMAN SCULPTURE *by Anna Maria Esposito*

The exhibition of Attic vases is accompanied by a small group of marble sculptures, including original Greek ones from Attica, Boethia and Oriental Greece (Greek cities on the coasts of Asia Minor): the two archaic kouroi *purchased for the Archaeological Museum by its first director Luigi Adriano Milani, the ionic* Head of a woman *and the fragment of funerary stele from the 4th century BC. The presence of these marble statues in Italy must be considered exceptional, and is linked to the despoiling of Greek sanctuaries and necropolises which began already in Roman times and continued through the centuries. Greek classical sculpture of the 5th and 4th centuries BC, known through marble replicas from Roman times, is represented here by a male torso, an athlete's head and a fragment of relief portraying the slaying of Niobe's children, and a re-elaboration in marble of the famous throne of Zeus by Phydias at Olympia, recently donated to the Museum by the Milani family.*

Head of a woman

c. 575-525 BC

Original of Greek-Oriental ambience
Coarse-grained white marble (insular Greek)
Height 25
Inv. no. 91226

The reading of the head, severely impaired by missing parts, must take account of the fact that the marble has been reworked around the eyes, the lips and in the area where a restored nose, later eliminated, has left the most devastating traces. These initiatives, which were obviously intended to reconstruct highly deteriorated features, show that the sculpture may have been included in a collection, perhaps that of the Florentine Grand Duchy, before entering the Archaeological Museum. The head, which belonged to a life-size statue, has been considered that of a woman also due to the presence of disc-shaped earrings. The hair, arranged in rows of long "beaded" braids, falls behind the large scroll-shaped ear.
A pair of thick braids rises above the mass of hair, introducing an element uncommon to the traditional archaic hairdo.

The elongated oval of the face and the rounded, fleshy chin, elements typical of Greek-insular sculpture, allow this statue to be attributed to one of these schools (perhaps that of Rhodes).

71

Statue of Kouros-Milani "Apollo"
(whole and details
on following page)

530 BC

White marble, probably
Parian. Attic production
Height 139
Inv. no. 99042

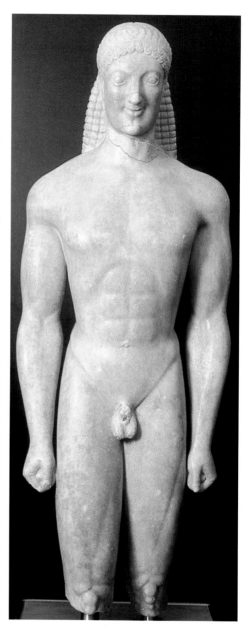

In archaic Greece (7ᵗʰ century BC) the nude male figure (*kouros*) and the draped female figure (*kore*) are the basic themes of monumental votive sculpture. The Greek artist "concentrates on man, conceived as [...] concrete image of universal order [...] the image of divinity made man. In this raising of man to the sphere of the ideal and this plunging of divinity into the human reality, the boundaries between human and divine aspect become blurred and in archaic monumental statuary the male figure nude and the female figure dressed, the *kouros* and the *kore*, remain indistinct in their ideal abstraction and can concretely express the two aspects [...]. The *kouroi* are known as *Apollini*, but it would be strange if Apollo were the only deity represented. We know in fact that the type is used also for victorious athletes as well as for offerers" (G. Becatti).

The Museum possesses

three archaic Greek originals: the female head and the two *kouroi* known as the *Milani Kouroi*, belonging since the 18th century to the collection of Canon Bellini of Osimo after having arrived in Italy, like so many Attic and insular marbles, as ballast for a ship.

The nose and mouth of the larger statue, with legs missing below the knee and head reattached, have been restored and integrated. This somewhat falsifies what must have been its origi-

nal features, accentuating the hardness of the face, characterized by great prominent eyes with the pupil and iris indicated and a mouth curving in the inevitable "archaic smile".

The elongated oval, with its prominent bone structure, is embellished on the forehead by an elaborate hair-do with corkscrew curls bound by a fillet. The thick hair falls in locks to the shoulders, broad and powerful, in contrast to the slender waistline.

The anatomical features on the torso and legs are indicated by grooves and incisions, rather than by contrasting volumes.

Statue of Kouros-Milani "Apollino"

530 BC
Coarse-grained marble
(insular Greek)
Attic production
Height 66
Inv. no. 99043

The small *Kouros* also belonged, like the larger one, to the collection of Cannon Bellini of Osimo and was purchased for the Museum by Luigi Adriano Milani.

"By contrast with the severity, the reserves and uncertainty of the critics in regard to the large *Kouros*, the smaller statue has always been the object of the most unconditional admiration. Undoubtedly, it is a very fine sculpture in which the tender forms and the subdued, vibrant modeling appeal immediately to those who find the rough and very personal language of the large *Kouros* too harsh and biting" (Enrico Paribeni).

The smooth, compact torso, the fluid outline and the soft forms are in sharp contrast to the angular incisiveness and analytic formulation of the structure in the larger *Kouros*, indicative not only of a different artistic personality and a chronological difference but also and above all of a different sphere of origin. Rather than Attica, in fact, the small statue finds its place "within the ambience of the Boethian *Kouroi*, sculptures which, as has been repeatedly noted, show continuous and always open relations with Cycladic sculpture".

Male torso

Roman copy of a Greek original
of the mid-5th century BC

Coarse white marble
(insular Greek).
Height 87
Inv. no. 13830

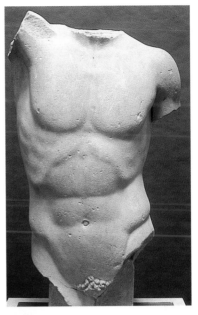

Roman copy of a Greek original
from the mid-5th century BC, this
Male torso, along with other replicas of the same statuary type,
recalls, for the right arm em-
phatically raised, the iconography of Perseus triumphantly waving aloft the Medusa's head.
The young, vigorous body is represented with a plastic sensiti-
vity now far from the schematic
solutions of archaic sculpture
and very near to the naturalism
of the fully Classical style.

Fragment of relief

2nd-1st century BC
Pentelic marble
Height 38;
length 58
Without Inv. no.

Donated in recent years
to the Archeological Mu-
seum by Elisa Frontali Milani, this work completes
the invaluable group of
Greek sculptures collec-
ted by Luigi Adriano Mi-
lani. The relief, which still
has a portion of its frame,
can be imagined as a pan-
el with two figures, a girl
running wildly, pieced by
a dart (the hole in which
the bronze dart was in-
serted still remains) and
a boy who has fallen to his
knees. The scene is easi-
ly recognizable as part of
the choral representation
of the killing of Niobe's
children by Artemis and
Apollo. This places the
fragment among the nu-
merous series of slabs of
marble carved in relief
(executed in Athenian
shops in late republican
and imperial times) which
represent, in friezes of a
certain size or "squares"
containing two figures (according to the neo-Attic
manner), larger or small-
er parts of the frieze that
decorated the throne of
Phidias' famous statue of
Zeus at Olympia.

GOLD-WORK *by Anna Maria Esposito*

The gold-work collection, which illustrates the evolution of the goldsmith's art for about fifteen centuries, from Etruscan orientalizing to the early Middle Ages, includes gold and silver pieces from the Medici-Lorraine Collections, first kept in the Uffizi and then moved to the Archaeological Museum (1890), as well as material acquired through purchases, donations and chance finding. The oldest core collection of gold-work left to the Uffizi Gallery by Cardinal Leopoldo de' Medici (1676) was enriched in the 18th century by the archeological material of the Galluzzi Collection of Volterra, and in the 19th century by the conspicuous legacy of jewelry and gemstones bequeathed by the englishmen William Currie. The sumptuous grave goods coming from excavations in the great Etruscan necropolises have instead been assigned to the Topographical Section of the Museum, temporarily closed to the public.

Cluster earrings

Second half of 4th century BC
Gold leaf with embossed decoration
Height 8.4
width 5.8
Inv. nos. 15803-15804

Found in 1820 during excavation to build a road between Orbetello and Grosseto, these gold leaves come from a pair of "cluster" earrings of a type very common in southern Etruria.

Basket earrings

Late 6th-early 7th century AD
Gold leaf and garnets
Height 3
Inv. nos. 15704-15705

Gold earrings of refined taste decorated with filigree and set with garnets, part of the legacy of William Currie, a gentleman from London who upon dying in 1863 left the Florentine Galleries his jewelry collection containing gold ornaments, cameo rings and engraved gemstones as well as gold and silver coins.

The very rich collection of gemstones and cameos was opened again to the public in 1990 on the second floor of Palazzo della Crocetta after having been closed for some 130 years. Since 1996 it has been placed in the long Medici Corridor, built to allow Maria Maddalena de' Medici, deformed since birth, to reach the church of Santissima Annunziata unseen.

The collection has very ancient origins: the first gemstones in it belonged to Cosimo the Elder and to Lorenzo de' Medici, who commissioned Ghiberti and Donatello to restore them, mount them and replicate them. This custom continued through the years. Tradition attributes to Benvenuto Cellini at least two pieces in the collection, which contains not only ancient pieces but also fine gemstones and cameos from the Renaissance and Baroque periods.

Cameo with Hermaphrodite

3rd century AD

White onyx on crystal background
Height 3; width 3.6
Inv. no. 14464

Cameo with gold frame enameled on front and back, set with four emeralds and four garnets. A semi-nude Hermaphrodite wearing armillae on his arm and sandals on his feet reclines limply against a rock covered by a lionskin, under a tree. He is surrounded by three cherubs; the first is waving a flabellum, the second is playing the pan-pipes, and the third the cithara. The transposition of this iconographic motif into glyptic works is attributed to Sostratos.

Cameo with Tiberius and Livia

Probably 17th century AD

Onyx on chalcedony
Height 5.8; width 4.8
Inv. no. 14533

Represented in the cameo surrounded by a fine gold fillet are Tiberius (crowned with laurel) and Livia (diadem ornamented with ears of grain and poppies), viewed from the right profile. Purchased by Cardinal Leopoldo de' Medici in 1674, the cameo was restored by Camelli.

Index

Printed in September 1999
at Giunti Industrie Grafiche S.p.A. – Prato